WILLIAM WALTON
arr. Tom Winpenny

MARCH FOR 'A HISTORY OF THE ENGLISH-SPEAKING PEOPLES'

OXFORD

March for 'A History of the English-Speaking Peoples'

WILLIAM WALTON
(1902–83)
arr. Tom Winpenny

Sw.: to Mixt. and Reed 8'
Gt.: Prin. 8', 4', 2', Sw. to Gt.
Ch.: Prin. 8', 4', 2', Sw. to Ch.

This arrangement was performed at the conclusion of the Service to Commemorate the 75th Anniversary of the Battle of Britain at St Paul's Cathedral, London, by Peter Holder on 15 September 2015. It has been recorded on the Regent and Priory labels.

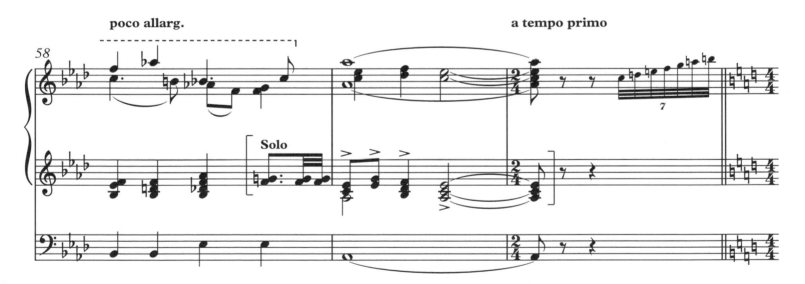

a tempo primo sub., più mosso

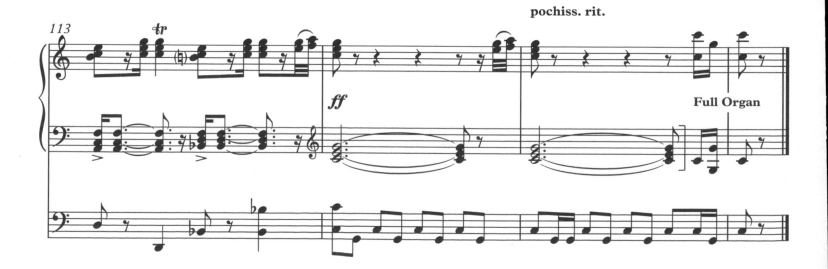